50 Wild Feast Dishes

By: Kelly Johnson

Table of Contents

- Roasted Wild Boar with Herb Glaze
- Grilled Venison Steaks with Berry Sauce
- Smoked Pheasant with Garlic Butter
- Wild Mushroom and Truffle Risotto
- Cedar-Planked Salmon with Maple Glaze
- Fire-Roasted Elk Burgers
- Foraged Herb and Root Vegetable Stew
- Stuffed Quail with Cranberry and Nuts
- Campfire-Grilled Trout with Lemon Butter
- Smoked Duck with Orange Glaze
- Wild Rabbit and Leek Pie
- Grilled Alligator Skewers
- Roasted Goose with Chestnut Stuffing
- Bison Short Ribs with Red Wine Reduction
- Braised Wild Hare with Juniper Berries
- Smoked Caribou Sausage
- Wood-Fired Wild Turkey with Honey Glaze
- Moose Stew with Root Vegetables
- Wild Berry and Nut Salad with Game Meat
- Spit-Roasted Whole Pig
- Wild Boar Ragu with Handmade Pasta
- Slow-Cooked Bear Roast
- Fire-Grilled Frog Legs with Garlic Butter
- Pigeon Pie with Mushroom Gravy
- Deep-Fried Rattlesnake Nuggets
- Elk Chili with Smoked Peppers
- Grilled Wild Sardines with Citrus Marinade
- Smoked Beaver Tail with Maple Syrup
- Roasted Hedgehog with Herbs
- Wild Rice and Duck Casserole
- Charcoal-Seared Octopus with Seaweed Salad
- Barbecued Python Skewers
- Slow-Cooked Kangaroo Stew
- Smoked Eel with Horseradish Cream
- Rustic Foraged Mushroom Soup

- Grilled Reindeer Steak with Lingonberry Sauce
- Barbecued Turtle Soup
- Venison Wellington with Puff Pastry
- Wild Boar Tacos with Pickled Onions
- Open-Flame Grilled Pheasant Breast
- Cured Wild Goose Prosciutto
- Braised Squirrel in Red Wine Sauce
- Forager's Nettle and Wild Herb Pesto Pasta
- Spicy Antelope Sausage Gumbo
- Slow-Roasted Beaver Stew
- Smoked Sturgeon with Dill Aioli
- Campfire-Cooked Muskrat with Vegetables
- Roasted Snails with Wild Garlic Butter
- Honey-Glazed Wild Duck Legs
- Rustic Acorn and Chestnut Bread with Wild Berries

Roasted Wild Boar with Herb Glaze

Ingredients:

- 3 lbs wild boar roast
- 2 tablespoons olive oil
- 3 cloves garlic, minced
- 1 tablespoon fresh rosemary, chopped
- 1 tablespoon fresh thyme, chopped
- 1 teaspoon salt
- 1/2 teaspoon black pepper
- 1/2 cup balsamic vinegar
- 2 tablespoons honey

Instructions:

1. Preheat the oven to 375°F (190°C).
2. Rub the wild boar roast with olive oil, garlic, rosemary, thyme, salt, and pepper.
3. Sear the roast in a hot skillet for three minutes per side.
4. Place in a roasting pan and cook for about one and a half hours, or until the internal temperature reaches 145°F (63°C).
5. In a saucepan, combine balsamic vinegar and honey. Simmer for five minutes until thickened.
6. Brush the glaze over the roast in the last 15 minutes of cooking.
7. Let rest for 10 minutes before slicing. Serve with roasted vegetables.

Grilled Venison Steaks with Berry Sauce

Ingredients:

- 4 venison steaks
- 2 tablespoons olive oil
- 1 teaspoon salt
- 1/2 teaspoon black pepper
- 1 teaspoon garlic powder
- 1 cup mixed berries (blueberries, raspberries, or blackberries)
- 1/2 cup red wine
- 2 tablespoons balsamic vinegar
- 1 tablespoon honey

Instructions:

1. Rub the venison steaks with olive oil, salt, pepper, and garlic powder.
2. Grill over medium-high heat for four minutes per side or until medium-rare.
3. In a saucepan, combine berries, red wine, balsamic vinegar, and honey. Simmer until reduced.
4. Strain the sauce if desired and drizzle over the grilled venison. Serve hot.

Smoked Pheasant with Garlic Butter

Ingredients:

- 1 whole pheasant
- 2 tablespoons butter, melted
- 3 cloves garlic, minced
- 1 teaspoon smoked paprika
- 1 teaspoon salt
- 1/2 teaspoon black pepper
- 1 cup wood chips (hickory or applewood)

Instructions:

1. Preheat the smoker to 225°F (107°C).
2. Rub the pheasant with melted butter, garlic, paprika, salt, and pepper.
3. Place wood chips in the smoker. Smoke the pheasant for about three hours until the internal temperature reaches 160°F (71°C).
4. Let rest for 10 minutes before carving. Serve with roasted potatoes.

Wild Mushroom and Truffle Risotto

Ingredients:

- 1 cup Arborio rice
- 4 cups chicken broth
- 1/2 cup white wine
- 1/2 cup wild mushrooms, chopped
- 1 tablespoon truffle oil
- 2 tablespoons butter
- 1/2 cup grated Parmesan
- 1/2 teaspoon salt
- 1/4 teaspoon black pepper

Instructions:

1. In a pan, melt the butter and sauté the mushrooms until soft.
2. Add the Arborio rice and cook for two minutes.
3. Pour in the white wine and stir until absorbed.
4. Gradually add the broth, stirring constantly, until the rice is tender.
5. Stir in Parmesan, truffle oil, salt, and pepper. Serve hot.

Cedar-Planked Salmon with Maple Glaze

Ingredients:

- 2 salmon fillets
- 1 cedar plank, soaked in water for one hour
- 2 tablespoons maple syrup
- 1 tablespoon Dijon mustard
- 1 tablespoon soy sauce
- 1/2 teaspoon black pepper

Instructions:

1. Preheat the grill to medium heat.
2. Place the salmon fillets on the cedar plank.
3. Mix the maple syrup, mustard, soy sauce, and pepper. Brush over the salmon.
4. Place the plank on the grill and cook for 15–20 minutes until the salmon flakes easily.
5. Serve with grilled vegetables or rice.

Fire-Roasted Elk Burgers

Ingredients:

- 1 pound ground elk meat
- 1/2 teaspoon salt
- 1/2 teaspoon black pepper
- 1/2 teaspoon smoked paprika
- 1 clove garlic, minced
- 1 tablespoon Worcestershire sauce
- 4 burger buns
- Toppings: lettuce, tomato, onion, cheese

Instructions:

1. Preheat the grill or campfire to medium-high heat.
2. Mix the elk meat with salt, pepper, paprika, garlic, and Worcestershire sauce. Form into patties.
3. Grill for three to four minutes per side until cooked through.
4. Serve on buns with toppings.

Foraged Herb and Root Vegetable Stew

Ingredients:

- 2 cups diced root vegetables (carrots, potatoes, parsnips)
- 1 onion, chopped
- 2 cloves garlic, minced
- 4 cups vegetable broth
- 1/2 teaspoon salt
- 1/2 teaspoon black pepper
- 1 teaspoon thyme
- 1/2 teaspoon rosemary
- 1 cup leafy greens (kale, spinach)

Instructions:

1. In a pot, sauté the onion and garlic until soft.
2. Add the root vegetables, broth, salt, pepper, thyme, and rosemary.
3. Simmer for 30 minutes until the vegetables are tender.
4. Stir in the leafy greens and cook for five more minutes. Serve warm.

Stuffed Quail with Cranberry and Nuts

Ingredients:

- 2 whole quails
- 1/2 cup cooked rice
- 1/4 cup dried cranberries
- 2 tablespoons chopped nuts (walnuts, almonds)
- 1 tablespoon butter, melted
- 1/2 teaspoon salt
- 1/4 teaspoon black pepper

Instructions:

1. Preheat the oven to 375°F (190°C).
2. Mix the rice, cranberries, nuts, butter, salt, and pepper.
3. Stuff the mixture into the quails and place them in a baking dish.
4. Roast for 25–30 minutes until golden brown and cooked through.
5. Let rest for five minutes before serving.

Campfire-Grilled Trout with Lemon Butter

Ingredients:

- 2 whole trout, cleaned
- 2 tablespoons butter, melted
- 1 lemon, sliced
- 2 cloves garlic, minced
- 1 teaspoon salt
- 1/2 teaspoon black pepper
- 1 teaspoon fresh parsley, chopped

Instructions:

1. Preheat a campfire or grill to medium heat.
2. Stuff the trout with lemon slices, garlic, and parsley.
3. Brush with melted butter and season with salt and pepper.
4. Grill for five to seven minutes per side until cooked through.
5. Serve with a squeeze of fresh lemon juice.

Smoked Duck with Orange Glaze

Ingredients:

- 1 whole duck
- 2 tablespoons olive oil
- 1 teaspoon salt
- 1/2 teaspoon black pepper
- 1 teaspoon smoked paprika
- 1 cup orange juice
- 1/4 cup honey
- 1 tablespoon soy sauce
- 1 tablespoon Dijon mustard
- Wood chips (applewood or hickory)

Instructions:

1. Preheat the smoker to 225°F (107°C).
2. Rub the duck with olive oil, salt, pepper, and smoked paprika.
3. Smoke the duck for about four hours until the internal temperature reaches 165°F (74°C).
4. In a saucepan, combine orange juice, honey, soy sauce, and mustard. Simmer until slightly thickened.
5. Brush the glaze over the duck in the last 30 minutes of smoking.
6. Let rest for 10 minutes before carving. Serve with roasted vegetables.

Wild Rabbit and Leek Pie

Ingredients:

- 2 rabbit legs, diced
- 2 leeks, chopped
- 1 onion, diced
- 2 cloves garlic, minced
- 2 tablespoons butter
- 1 cup chicken broth
- 1/2 cup heavy cream
- 1 teaspoon thyme
- 1/2 teaspoon salt
- 1/4 teaspoon black pepper
- 1 sheet puff pastry
- 1 egg, beaten (for egg wash)

Instructions:

1. Preheat the oven to 375°F (190°C).
2. In a pan, melt butter and sauté leeks, onion, and garlic until soft.
3. Add the rabbit, broth, cream, thyme, salt, and pepper. Simmer for 20 minutes.
4. Transfer to a baking dish, cover with puff pastry, and brush with egg wash.
5. Bake for 25–30 minutes until golden brown. Serve warm.

Grilled Alligator Skewers

Ingredients:

- 1 lb alligator meat, cubed
- 2 tablespoons olive oil
- 1 teaspoon Cajun seasoning
- 1/2 teaspoon salt
- 1/4 teaspoon black pepper
- 1 bell pepper, chopped
- 1 onion, chopped
- 1 lemon, sliced
- Wooden skewers (soaked in water for 30 minutes)

Instructions:

1. Preheat the grill to medium-high heat.
2. Toss alligator meat with olive oil, Cajun seasoning, salt, and pepper.
3. Thread alligator, bell pepper, and onion onto skewers.
4. Grill for 4–5 minutes per side until cooked through.
5. Serve with lemon slices and a dipping sauce of choice.

Roasted Goose with Chestnut Stuffing

Ingredients:

- 1 whole goose
- 2 tablespoons butter, melted
- 1 teaspoon salt
- 1/2 teaspoon black pepper
- 1 teaspoon sage
- 1 teaspoon thyme
- 1 cup chestnuts, chopped
- 1/2 cup breadcrumbs
- 1/2 cup chicken broth
- 1/4 cup dried cranberries

Instructions:

1. Preheat the oven to 350°F (175°C).
2. Rub the goose with butter, salt, pepper, sage, and thyme.
3. In a bowl, mix chestnuts, breadcrumbs, broth, and cranberries. Stuff the goose.
4. Roast for 2–3 hours until the internal temperature reaches 165°F (74°C).
5. Let rest for 15 minutes before carving.

Bison Short Ribs with Red Wine Reduction

Ingredients:

- 2 lbs bison short ribs
- 2 tablespoons olive oil
- 1 teaspoon salt
- 1/2 teaspoon black pepper
- 1 onion, chopped
- 2 cloves garlic, minced
- 1 cup red wine
- 2 cups beef broth
- 1 sprig rosemary

Instructions:

1. Preheat the oven to 325°F (163°C).
2. Season short ribs with salt and pepper. Sear in olive oil until browned.
3. Add onion and garlic, cooking until softened.
4. Pour in red wine and broth. Add rosemary.
5. Cover and braise for 3 hours until tender. Serve with mashed potatoes.

Braised Wild Hare with Juniper Berries

Ingredients:

- 2 wild hare legs
- 2 tablespoons olive oil
- 1 onion, chopped
- 2 cloves garlic, minced
- 1 cup red wine
- 1 cup beef broth
- 1 teaspoon juniper berries, crushed
- 1/2 teaspoon thyme
- 1/2 teaspoon salt

Instructions:

1. Sear the hare legs in olive oil until browned.
2. Add onion, garlic, wine, broth, juniper berries, thyme, and salt.
3. Cover and braise on low heat for 2 hours until tender.
4. Serve with roasted root vegetables.

Smoked Caribou Sausage

Ingredients:

- 1 lb ground caribou meat
- 1/2 lb ground pork fat
- 1 teaspoon salt
- 1/2 teaspoon black pepper
- 1/2 teaspoon smoked paprika
- 1/2 teaspoon garlic powder
- Natural sausage casings
- Wood chips (hickory or applewood)

Instructions:

1. Mix caribou meat, pork fat, salt, pepper, paprika, and garlic powder.
2. Stuff into sausage casings and twist into links.
3. Preheat the smoker to 200°F (93°C) and add wood chips.
4. Smoke for 3–4 hours until the internal temperature reaches 160°F (71°C).
5. Let rest before slicing and serving.

Wood-Fired Wild Turkey with Honey Glaze

Ingredients:

- 1 whole wild turkey
- 3 tablespoons butter, melted
- 1 teaspoon salt
- 1/2 teaspoon black pepper
- 1/2 teaspoon smoked paprika
- 1/4 cup honey
- 2 tablespoons Dijon mustard

Instructions:

1. Preheat a wood-fired oven or grill to 350°F (175°C).
2. Rub the turkey with butter, salt, pepper, and paprika.
3. Roast for 2–3 hours, basting occasionally.
4. Mix honey and mustard, and brush onto the turkey in the last 30 minutes of roasting.
5. Let rest for 15 minutes before carving.

Moose Stew with Root Vegetables

Ingredients:

- 2 lbs moose meat, cubed
- 2 tablespoons olive oil
- 1 onion, chopped
- 2 cloves garlic, minced
- 4 cups beef broth
- 2 carrots, chopped
- 2 potatoes, cubed
- 1 teaspoon thyme
- 1/2 teaspoon salt
- 1/4 teaspoon black pepper

Instructions:

1. Sear moose meat in olive oil until browned.
2. Add onion, garlic, and broth. Simmer for 1 hour.
3. Add carrots, potatoes, thyme, salt, and pepper. Cook until tender.
4. Serve hot with crusty bread.

Wild Berry and Nut Salad with Game Meat

Ingredients:

- 2 cups mixed greens
- 1/2 cup wild berries (blueberries, raspberries, or blackberries)
- 1/4 cup chopped nuts (walnuts, almonds)
- 1/4 cup goat cheese, crumbled
- 1 grilled venison steak, sliced
- 2 tablespoons balsamic vinaigrette

Instructions:

1. Toss greens, berries, nuts, and goat cheese in a bowl.
2. Slice the grilled venison steak and place on top.
3. Drizzle with balsamic vinaigrette and serve.

Spit-Roasted Whole Pig

Ingredients:

- 1 whole pig (30-50 lbs)
- 1/2 cup sea salt
- 1/4 cup black pepper
- 1/4 cup garlic powder
- 1/4 cup smoked paprika
- 1/2 cup olive oil
- 1/4 cup apple cider vinegar
- 2 tablespoons dried oregano
- 1 tablespoon cayenne pepper
- 1/2 cup lemon juice

Instructions:

1. Prepare the pig by cleaning and drying it thoroughly.
2. Rub the entire pig with olive oil, followed by a mixture of salt, pepper, garlic powder, smoked paprika, oregano, and cayenne.
3. Secure the pig on a spit and start roasting over an open flame at low heat (250-300°F).
4. Baste occasionally with a mix of lemon juice and apple cider vinegar.
5. Roast for 6-8 hours, rotating constantly, until the internal temperature reaches 190°F.
6. Let rest for 30 minutes before carving.

Wild Boar Ragu with Handmade Pasta

Ingredients:

- 2 lbs wild boar shoulder, diced
- 1 onion, chopped
- 2 cloves garlic, minced
- 1 carrot, diced
- 1 celery stalk, diced
- 2 cups crushed tomatoes
- 1 cup red wine
- 1 cup beef broth
- 1 teaspoon rosemary
- 1 teaspoon thyme
- 1 teaspoon salt
- 1/2 teaspoon black pepper
- 1 lb handmade pasta (pappardelle or tagliatelle)

Instructions:

1. Sear wild boar in a Dutch oven until browned.
2. Add onion, garlic, carrot, and celery. Sauté until softened.
3. Pour in red wine, deglazing the pot.
4. Add crushed tomatoes, broth, rosemary, thyme, salt, and pepper.
5. Simmer for 2-3 hours until tender.
6. Cook pasta and serve with the ragu.

Slow-Cooked Bear Roast

Ingredients:

- 3 lbs bear roast
- 2 tablespoons olive oil
- 1 onion, sliced
- 2 cloves garlic, minced
- 2 cups beef broth
- 1 cup red wine
- 2 carrots, chopped
- 2 potatoes, cubed
- 1 teaspoon thyme
- 1 teaspoon salt
- 1/2 teaspoon black pepper

Instructions:

1. Sear bear roast in olive oil until browned on all sides.
2. Place in a slow cooker with onions, garlic, broth, wine, carrots, and potatoes.
3. Season with thyme, salt, and pepper.
4. Cook on low for 8-10 hours until tender.
5. Slice and serve with vegetables.

Fire-Grilled Frog Legs with Garlic Butter

Ingredients:

- 12 frog legs
- 3 tablespoons butter, melted
- 2 cloves garlic, minced
- 1 tablespoon lemon juice
- 1 teaspoon salt
- 1/2 teaspoon black pepper
- 1/2 teaspoon cayenne pepper

Instructions:

1. Preheat grill to medium heat.
2. Mix butter, garlic, lemon juice, salt, pepper, and cayenne.
3. Brush frog legs with the garlic butter mixture.
4. Grill for 2-3 minutes per side.
5. Serve hot with extra garlic butter.

Pigeon Pie with Mushroom Gravy

Ingredients:

- 4 pigeon breasts, diced
- 1 onion, chopped
- 2 cloves garlic, minced
- 1 cup mushrooms, sliced
- 2 tablespoons butter
- 1 cup chicken broth
- 1/2 cup heavy cream
- 1 teaspoon thyme
- 1/2 teaspoon salt
- 1/4 teaspoon black pepper
- 1 sheet puff pastry
- 1 egg (for egg wash)

Instructions:

1. Preheat oven to 375°F.
2. Sauté pigeon meat in butter until browned. Add onions, garlic, and mushrooms.
3. Pour in broth and cream. Add thyme, salt, and pepper. Simmer until thickened.
4. Transfer to a pie dish, cover with puff pastry, and brush with egg wash.
5. Bake for 25-30 minutes until golden brown.

Deep-Fried Rattlesnake Nuggets

Ingredients:

- 1 lb rattlesnake meat, cubed
- 1 cup buttermilk
- 1 cup flour
- 1 teaspoon paprika
- 1 teaspoon garlic powder
- 1/2 teaspoon salt
- 1/4 teaspoon black pepper
- Vegetable oil for frying

Instructions:

1. Soak rattlesnake meat in buttermilk for 30 minutes.
2. Mix flour, paprika, garlic powder, salt, and pepper.
3. Heat oil to 350°F.
4. Dredge meat in flour mixture and fry until golden brown.
5. Serve with dipping sauce.

Elk Chili with Smoked Peppers

Ingredients:

- 1 lb ground elk
- 1 onion, diced
- 2 cloves garlic, minced
- 2 cups diced tomatoes
- 1 cup kidney beans
- 1 cup black beans
- 1 cup smoked bell peppers, chopped
- 2 cups beef broth
- 1 teaspoon cumin
- 1 teaspoon chili powder
- 1/2 teaspoon salt

Instructions:

1. Brown elk meat with onions and garlic.
2. Add tomatoes, beans, smoked peppers, broth, and spices.
3. Simmer for 1-2 hours. Serve hot.

Grilled Wild Sardines with Citrus Marinade

Ingredients:

- 8 whole sardines
- 2 tablespoons olive oil
- 1 tablespoon lemon juice
- 1 tablespoon orange juice
- 1 teaspoon salt
- 1/2 teaspoon black pepper

Instructions:

1. Mix olive oil, lemon juice, orange juice, salt, and pepper.
2. Marinate sardines for 30 minutes.
3. Grill for 3 minutes per side.
4. Serve with fresh lemon wedges.

Smoked Beaver Tail with Maple Syrup

Ingredients:

- 1 beaver tail
- 2 tablespoons olive oil
- 1 teaspoon salt
- 1/2 teaspoon black pepper
- 1/4 cup maple syrup

Instructions:

1. Preheat smoker to 225°F.
2. Rub beaver tail with olive oil, salt, and pepper.
3. Smoke for 2-3 hours.
4. Brush with maple syrup in the last 30 minutes.

Roasted Hedgehog with Herbs

Ingredients:

- 1 whole hedgehog, cleaned
- 2 tablespoons olive oil
- 1 teaspoon salt
- 1/2 teaspoon black pepper
- 1 teaspoon rosemary
- 1 teaspoon thyme

Instructions:

1. Preheat oven to 350°F.
2. Rub hedgehog with olive oil, salt, pepper, rosemary, and thyme.
3. Roast for 1-2 hours until tender.

Wild Rice and Duck Casserole

Ingredients:

- 2 duck breasts, diced
- 1 cup wild rice
- 2 cups chicken broth
- 1 onion, chopped
- 2 cloves garlic, minced
- 1 cup mushrooms, sliced
- 1/2 cup heavy cream
- 1 teaspoon salt
- 1/2 teaspoon black pepper

Instructions:

1. Preheat oven to 375°F.
2. Sauté duck, onions, and garlic.
3. Mix with wild rice, broth, mushrooms, cream, salt, and pepper in a baking dish.
4. Bake for 40 minutes.

Charcoal-Seared Octopus with Seaweed Salad

Ingredients:

- 2 lbs octopus, cleaned
- 2 tablespoons olive oil
- 1 teaspoon sea salt
- 1/2 teaspoon black pepper
- 1 teaspoon smoked paprika
- 1 tablespoon lemon juice
- 1 cup mixed seaweed, rehydrated
- 1 tablespoon sesame oil
- 1 teaspoon soy sauce
- 1 teaspoon rice vinegar

Instructions:

1. Bring a large pot of salted water to a boil and simmer the octopus for 45 minutes until tender.
2. Remove and let cool, then cut into large chunks.
3. Brush octopus with olive oil, salt, pepper, and paprika.
4. Sear over hot charcoal for 1-2 minutes per side.
5. Toss seaweed with sesame oil, soy sauce, and rice vinegar.
6. Serve seared octopus with seaweed salad and a drizzle of lemon juice.

Barbecued Python Skewers

Ingredients:

- 1 lb python meat, cubed
- 2 tablespoons soy sauce
- 1 tablespoon honey
- 1 teaspoon garlic powder
- 1 teaspoon smoked paprika
- 1/2 teaspoon black pepper
- 1/2 teaspoon salt
- 1 tablespoon lemon juice
- Wooden skewers, soaked in water

Instructions:

1. Marinate python meat in soy sauce, honey, garlic powder, paprika, salt, and lemon juice for 2 hours.
2. Thread onto skewers and grill over medium-high heat for 5-6 minutes, turning occasionally.
3. Serve hot with a side of grilled vegetables.

Slow-Cooked Kangaroo Stew

Ingredients:

- 2 lbs kangaroo meat, cubed
- 1 onion, chopped
- 2 cloves garlic, minced
- 2 carrots, chopped
- 2 potatoes, cubed
- 4 cups beef broth
- 1 cup red wine
- 1 teaspoon thyme
- 1 teaspoon rosemary
- 1 teaspoon salt
- 1/2 teaspoon black pepper

Instructions:

1. Sear kangaroo meat in a Dutch oven until browned.
2. Add onions, garlic, carrots, and potatoes.
3. Pour in beef broth and red wine. Add thyme, rosemary, salt, and pepper.
4. Simmer on low heat for 3-4 hours until tender.
5. Serve with crusty bread.

Smoked Eel with Horseradish Cream

Ingredients:

- 2 whole eels, cleaned
- 1 teaspoon sea salt
- 1/2 teaspoon black pepper
- 1 teaspoon smoked paprika
- 2 tablespoons olive oil
- 1/2 cup sour cream
- 1 tablespoon horseradish
- 1 teaspoon lemon juice

Instructions:

1. Rub eels with olive oil, salt, pepper, and smoked paprika.
2. Smoke at 225°F for 3 hours until tender.
3. Mix sour cream, horseradish, and lemon juice for the sauce.
4. Serve smoked eel with horseradish cream.

Rustic Foraged Mushroom Soup

Ingredients:

- 2 cups mixed wild mushrooms, sliced
- 1 onion, chopped
- 2 cloves garlic, minced
- 2 tablespoons butter
- 4 cups vegetable broth
- 1/2 cup heavy cream
- 1 teaspoon thyme
- 1/2 teaspoon salt
- 1/4 teaspoon black pepper

Instructions:

1. Sauté mushrooms, onion, and garlic in butter until soft.
2. Add broth, thyme, salt, and pepper. Simmer for 20 minutes.
3. Stir in heavy cream and serve hot.

Grilled Reindeer Steak with Lingonberry Sauce

Ingredients:

- 2 reindeer steaks
- 1 tablespoon olive oil
- 1 teaspoon salt
- 1/2 teaspoon black pepper
- 1/2 teaspoon smoked paprika
- 1/2 cup lingonberry jam
- 1 tablespoon balsamic vinegar

Instructions:

1. Rub steaks with olive oil, salt, pepper, and smoked paprika.
2. Grill over medium-high heat for 4-5 minutes per side.
3. Mix lingonberry jam with balsamic vinegar and warm slightly.
4. Serve steaks with lingonberry sauce.

Barbecued Turtle Soup

Ingredients:

- 2 lbs turtle meat, cubed
- 1 onion, chopped
- 2 cloves garlic, minced
- 2 carrots, chopped
- 2 stalks celery, chopped
- 4 cups beef broth
- 1 cup diced tomatoes
- 1 teaspoon Worcestershire sauce
- 1 teaspoon salt
- 1/2 teaspoon black pepper

Instructions:

1. Sear turtle meat in a pot until browned.
2. Add onions, garlic, carrots, and celery.
3. Pour in broth, tomatoes, Worcestershire sauce, salt, and pepper.
4. Simmer for 2-3 hours until tender.
5. Serve hot.

Venison Wellington with Puff Pastry

Ingredients:

- 1 venison loin
- 2 tablespoons olive oil
- 1 teaspoon salt
- 1/2 teaspoon black pepper
- 1 cup mushrooms, finely chopped
- 2 tablespoons butter
- 1 sheet puff pastry
- 1 egg (for egg wash)

Instructions:

1. Sear venison in olive oil until browned.
2. Sauté mushrooms in butter and cool.
3. Wrap venison in puff pastry with mushrooms.
4. Brush with egg wash and bake at 375°F for 25 minutes.

Wild Boar Tacos with Pickled Onions

Ingredients:

- 1 lb wild boar shoulder, shredded
- 1 teaspoon cumin
- 1 teaspoon smoked paprika
- 1/2 teaspoon salt
- 1/2 teaspoon black pepper
- 8 small tortillas
- 1/2 cup pickled onions

Instructions:

1. Slow-cook wild boar with seasonings for 4 hours until tender.
2. Serve in tortillas with pickled onions.

Open-Flame Grilled Pheasant Breast

Ingredients:

- 2 pheasant breasts
- 1 tablespoon olive oil
- 1 teaspoon salt
- 1/2 teaspoon black pepper
- 1/2 teaspoon garlic powder

Instructions:

1. Rub pheasant with olive oil and seasonings.
2. Grill over open flame for 4-5 minutes per side.

Cured Wild Goose Prosciutto

Ingredients:

- 2 wild goose breasts
- 1/2 cup sea salt
- 1/2 teaspoon black pepper
- 1 teaspoon rosemary
- 1 teaspoon thyme

Instructions:

1. Coat goose breasts in salt, pepper, rosemary, and thyme.
2. Wrap in cheesecloth and hang in a cool, dry place for 3 weeks.
3. Slice thin and serve.

Braised Squirrel in Red Wine Sauce

Ingredients:

- 2 squirrels, cleaned and cut into pieces
- 2 tablespoons olive oil
- 1 onion, chopped
- 2 cloves garlic, minced
- 1 carrot, chopped
- 2 cups red wine
- 2 cups beef broth
- 1 teaspoon thyme
- 1 teaspoon rosemary
- 1 teaspoon salt
- 1/2 teaspoon black pepper

Instructions:

1. Heat olive oil in a Dutch oven and brown the squirrel pieces.
2. Remove and sauté onion, garlic, and carrot until soft.
3. Return squirrel to the pot and add red wine and beef broth.
4. Stir in thyme, rosemary, salt, and pepper.
5. Cover and simmer on low for 2-3 hours until tender.
6. Serve with mashed potatoes or crusty bread.

Forager's Nettle and Wild Herb Pesto Pasta

Ingredients:

- 2 cups fresh nettles (blanched and drained)
- 1/2 cup wild herbs (dandelion, sorrel, or parsley)
- 1/2 cup walnuts
- 1/2 cup grated Parmesan
- 2 cloves garlic
- 1/2 cup olive oil
- 1 teaspoon lemon juice
- Salt and pepper to taste
- 1 lb pasta

Instructions:

1. Blend nettles, herbs, walnuts, Parmesan, garlic, olive oil, and lemon juice until smooth.
2. Season with salt and pepper.
3. Cook pasta according to package instructions and toss with pesto.
4. Serve with extra Parmesan on top.

Spicy Antelope Sausage Gumbo

Ingredients:

- 1 lb antelope sausage, sliced
- 1 onion, chopped
- 2 celery stalks, chopped
- 1 bell pepper, chopped
- 3 cloves garlic, minced
- 4 cups chicken broth
- 1 can diced tomatoes
- 1 teaspoon smoked paprika
- 1 teaspoon cayenne pepper
- 1 teaspoon thyme
- 1 teaspoon salt
- 1/2 teaspoon black pepper
- 1/2 cup flour
- 1/2 cup butter
- 1 lb shrimp (optional)
- 3 cups cooked rice

Instructions:

1. In a large pot, make a roux by stirring butter and flour over medium heat until golden brown.
2. Add sausage, onion, celery, bell pepper, and garlic. Cook until softened.
3. Stir in broth, tomatoes, paprika, cayenne, thyme, salt, and pepper.
4. Simmer for 1 hour, adding shrimp in the last 10 minutes if using.
5. Serve over rice.

Slow-Roasted Beaver Stew

Ingredients:

- 2 lbs beaver meat, cubed
- 1 onion, chopped
- 2 cloves garlic, minced
- 2 carrots, chopped
- 2 potatoes, cubed
- 4 cups beef broth
- 1 cup red wine
- 1 teaspoon thyme
- 1 teaspoon salt
- 1/2 teaspoon black pepper

Instructions:

1. Brown beaver meat in a Dutch oven.
2. Add onions, garlic, carrots, and potatoes.
3. Pour in broth and wine. Add thyme, salt, and pepper.
4. Cover and roast at 300°F for 4 hours until tender.
5. Serve with crusty bread.

Smoked Sturgeon with Dill Aioli

Ingredients:

- 2 sturgeon fillets
- 1 teaspoon sea salt
- 1/2 teaspoon black pepper
- 1 teaspoon smoked paprika
- 2 tablespoons olive oil
- 1/2 cup mayonnaise
- 1 tablespoon chopped dill
- 1 teaspoon lemon juice
- 1 teaspoon garlic powder

Instructions:

1. Rub sturgeon fillets with olive oil, salt, pepper, and smoked paprika.
2. Smoke at 225°F for 2 hours until flaky.
3. Mix mayonnaise, dill, lemon juice, and garlic powder for the aioli.
4. Serve smoked sturgeon with dill aioli on the side.

Campfire-Cooked Muskrat with Vegetables

Ingredients:

- 2 muskrats, cleaned and quartered
- 2 tablespoons olive oil
- 1 onion, chopped
- 2 carrots, sliced
- 2 potatoes, cubed
- 4 cups chicken broth
- 1 teaspoon salt
- 1/2 teaspoon black pepper
- 1 teaspoon thyme

Instructions:

1. Heat oil in a cast-iron pot over a campfire and brown muskrat pieces.
2. Add onion, carrots, and potatoes.
3. Pour in broth and season with salt, pepper, and thyme.
4. Cover and cook for 2 hours until tender.

Roasted Snails with Wild Garlic Butter

Ingredients:

- 12 snails, cleaned
- 1/2 cup butter, softened
- 2 tablespoons wild garlic, minced
- 1 teaspoon lemon juice
- 1/2 teaspoon salt
- 1/4 teaspoon black pepper

Instructions:

1. Preheat oven to 375°F.
2. Mix butter, wild garlic, lemon juice, salt, and pepper.
3. Place snails in shells and top with garlic butter.
4. Roast for 10 minutes and serve warm.

Honey-Glazed Wild Duck Legs

Ingredients:

- 4 wild duck legs
- 2 tablespoons honey
- 1 tablespoon soy sauce
- 1 teaspoon Dijon mustard
- 1/2 teaspoon black pepper
- 1/2 teaspoon salt

Instructions:

1. Preheat oven to 375°F.
2. Mix honey, soy sauce, mustard, salt, and pepper.
3. Brush duck legs with glaze.
4. Roast for 1 hour, basting every 20 minutes.

Rustic Acorn and Chestnut Bread with Wild Berries

Ingredients:

- 1 cup acorn flour
- 1 cup chestnut flour
- 1 cup all-purpose flour
- 1 teaspoon baking powder
- 1/2 teaspoon salt
- 1/4 cup honey
- 1 cup milk
- 1/2 cup wild berries

Instructions:

1. Preheat oven to 350°F.
2. Mix all flours, baking powder, and salt.
3. Stir in honey and milk until combined.
4. Fold in wild berries.
5. Bake for 40 minutes until golden brown.

www.ingramcontent.com/pod-product-compliance
Lightning Source LLC
LaVergne TN
LVHW081507060526
838201LV00056BA/2981